THE GUIDED Gratitude Journal

CULTIVATE THE GRATITUDE HABIT WITH A 5 MINUTE DAILY JOURNAL FEATURING QUICK MINDFULNESS PROMPTS FOR LASTING JOY.

This Journal Belongs To

"

The more you practice the art of thankfulness, the more you have to be thankful for.

- NORMAN VINCENT PEALE

"

Your Gift

AS A THANK YOU FOR GETTING THIS JOURNAL WE'D LIKE TO ALSO OFFER YOU: SCAN THE CODE TO GET YOUR COPY

100 GRATITUDE PROMPTS:

Keep your gratitude habit as powerful as possible with this mini book of amazing gratitude prompts.

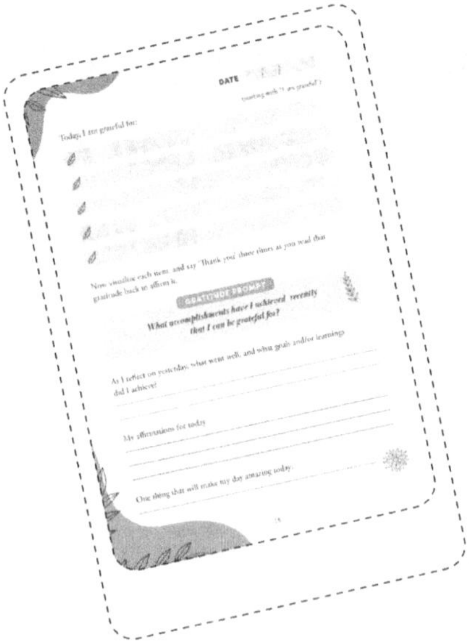

MORE GRATITUDE TEMPLATES :

Keep your gratitude habit going with even more daily templates for you to use.

Who are Manifestation Pulse

Manifestation Pulse are a dedicated team of manifestation coaches who have been working with hundreds of clients worldwide for the last 3 years to help them manifest what they truly desire.

Why Gratitude Matters

The fundamental principle governing our reality is that energy is the building block of existence. Your body is a mass of energy. The table you eat on, the chair you may be sitting on, and everything around you is ultimately composed of energy.

The law of attraction states that like attracts like. This means that you attract the energy that is in harmony with you. The difference between attracting positive or negative things is the vibrational frequency you are in.

Gratitude is at the heart of the work that we do in order to help our clients raise their vibrational frequency (or "high vibe" as we call it), and it's the reason that we've put this guided gratitude journal together for you.

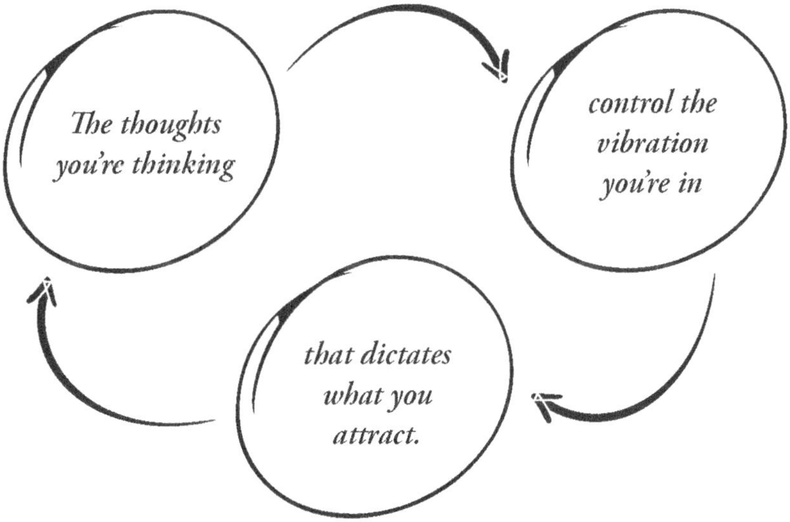

Another thing about the Law of Attraction - it's **always** working, like the law of gravity! Beyond being in a high vibration, there are many benefits to gratitude journalling including:

- **IMPROVED SLEEP QUALITY.**
- **HAPPIER FOR OTHERS' SUCCESS.**
- **FORM HEALTHY HABITS.**
- **BECOME MORE SATISFIED IN OUR RELATIONSHIPS.**
- **INCREASE RESILIENCE AND LOWER STRESS.**
- **BE MORE CONNECTED TO OURSELVES.**
- **IMPROVE SELF ESTEEM.**
- **EASE THE SYMPTOMS OF DEPRESSION.**

This journal isn't just a template for you to fill in everyday. Instead we'll be taking you on a journey - to make sure that your mind is in its highest vibration so that you can truly attract what you desire most, and be grateful and mindful of what you already have around you.

You can get more daily ideas and inspiration on our TikTok channel here.

How to use this Journal

YOUR GRATITUDE JOURNEY

When you start a car, you don't put the car into 5th gear straight away. You warm it up. That's exactly what we're going to do here, by putting you through the gears of gratitude.

The Warm up: In days 1 - 7 we'll be opening up your mind to different ways of thinking about gratitude so that you have a foundation in the days after. Whether you're new to gratitude or have been practicing for some time, this section is an important foundation.

The Habit: We will then work through 100 days of gratitude, with prompts that not only keep your gratitude habit consistent, but also allow you to widen your capacity for gratitude, and help you achieve your highest vibration.

The Reflection: We will also check in from time to time and make gratitude days an important point to reflect on things.

Reflection Point

Along the way, we'll sprinkle a few sage words from those who have been on this path and taught many more.

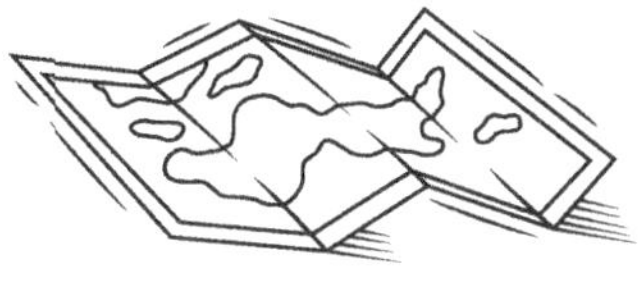

FAQ

"Do I have to journal everyday?" This is one of the frequently asked questions we get a lot. The answer is no. You don't. For some, getting into the daily habit is important to them, but some studies suggest that writing in a gratitude journal three times per week might actually have a greater impact on our happiness than journalling every day - so we recommend at least three times in a week.

A few tips before we get started:

1. Keep this journal in plain sight - so it's a constant reminder to you.
2. Mark your calendar with the days of the week that you want to devote to your gratitude journal.
3. Find a quiet space to write - choose a consistent space whether indoors or outdoors.
4. Journal during the day or night - whatever feels right for you.
5. Feel the feels - when you're writing in your gratitude journal, don't just note the words down – ensure that you're feeling the emotions of gratitude, appreciation and joy in your body as strongly as you can.

Are you ready?

THEN LET'S GET INTO THE GROOVE!

Day One

LET'S START BY GETTING INTO THE RIGHT MINDSET.

DATE / /

Write down 3 small and simple things that bring a smile to you - 3 things that bring happiness and pleasure. These don't need to be 'big' things, but can also be everyday simple pleasures like getting a particular coffee in the morning, the sun beaming through your windows, the sound of nature, or any specific creation you love seeing - even if only momentarily in the day. Along with those things, write down WHY you're grateful, and start each sentence with "I am grateful for."
E.g. I am grateful for my iced latte first thing in the morning, because of the energy and focus it brings to me.

When you have your 3 - visualize each item, and say 'Thank you' 3 times for each one as you read that gratitude back to affirm it.

> **"Gratitude is the currency of the manifesting world. In order to attract more, we must express gratitude for what we."**

Great work
you've taken your first step into the gratitude mindset. Looking forward to seeing you on Day 2 already.

Day Two

WHO ARE YOU GRATEFUL FOR?

DATE / /

Write down 5 people who you are grateful for, and why.
Start each sentence with "I am grateful for" and why just like on Day One.

Now visualize each of these people, and say 'Thank you' three times as you read that gratitude back to affirm it.

"

Gratitude is the ability to experience life as a gift. It liberates us from the prison of self-preoccupation.

- JOHN ORTBERG

"

Day Three

LOOKING FORWARD TO LOOK BACK

DATE / /

What is something you are looking forward to tomorrow? It might be an important meeting, a meet up with a friend or new connection, or it might just be getting something new from the shops. No matter how big or small it may seem, what is it that you are looking forward to?

What are 4 things you are looking forward to by this time next week?

Now visualize each item, and say 'Thank you' three times as you read that gratitude back to affirm it.

Gratitude makes sense of our past, brings peace for today, and creates a vision for tomorrow.

- MELODY BEATTIE

Day Four

WHAT ARE YOUR GOALS?

DATE / /

Close your eyes, and think about your goals - what are they? What is it you truly desire?

What 5 things do you truly desire? Write each one as an affirmation. E.g. if you want to be financially free, write "I am grateful to be on a path to financial freedom."

Now visualize each item, and say 'Thank you' three times as you read that gratitude back to affirm it.

Did you enjoy what you were looking forward to yesterday? Why?

"

Never let the things you want make you forget the things you have.

- SANCHITA PANDEY

"

Day Five

THERE'S BEAUTY, EVERYWHERE

DATE / /

What moments of beauty or wonder have you experienced recently that you are grateful for? Has there been a recent experience that has brought you joy or laughter? If you want to do this closer to home, close your eyes and "Walk around" your home in your mind…and think of all the lovely things that you really value.

What 5 moments of wonder or things in your home are you grateful for and why?

Appreciation is a wonderful thing. It makes what is excellent in others belong to us as well.

- VOLTAIRE

Day Six

COUNT YOUR LUCKY STARS

DATE / /

What are 5 times you can recall when unexpected blessings came into your life? These blessings could be money, random people and connections, or other moments that felt serendipitous.

Now visualize each item, and say 'Thank you' three times as you read that gratitude back to affirm it.

> *Gratitude is the most exquisite form of courtesy.*
>
> **- JACQUES MARITAIN**

Day Seven

DEAR ME, LOVE FROM ME

DATE / /

Write a letter to yourself from the future. What aspects of yourself are you grateful for? For instance, what are the ways that you have shown up for yourself? What are the things you've done that you're especially proud of, or behavior you've taken that really makes you, you?

Write 3 affirmations or today. Starting with "I am"

E.g. I am so lucky. Everything works out for me. Miracles happen to me daily.

"Gratitude is one of the most powerful human emotions. Once expressed, it changes attitude, brightens outlook and broadens our perspective.

- GERMANY KENT"

Great work
you have built your gratitude foundation! Now let's make it a habit .

100 days of gratitude

Across the next 100 days of gratitude, we're going to ask you what 5 things you are grateful for. Use your learnings from the first 7 days, and think laterally about the things, people, experiences, and joys that you are truly grateful for. For each day, we'll include a little prompt to help you think as expansively as possible.

We'll also ask you to reflect on the previous day, as well as the 1 thing that is going to make your present day amazing. Finally, we'll create room for you to write down affirmations that really mean something to you.

DATE / /

Today, I am grateful for: (starting with "I am grateful")

Now visualize each item, and say 'Thank you' three times as you read that gratitude back to affirm it.

GRATITUDE PROMPT

What accomplishments have I achieved recently that I can be grateful for?

As I reflect on yesterday, what went well, and what goals and/or learnings did I achieve?

My affirmations for today:

One thing that will make my day amazing today:

DATE / /

Today, I am grateful for: (starting with "I am grateful")

Now visualize each item, and say 'Thank you' three times as you read that gratitude back to affirm it.

GRATITUDE PROMPT

Who has supported me on my journey?

As I reflect on yesterday, what went well, and what goals and/or learnings did I achieve?

My affirmations for today:

One thing that will make my day amazing today:

DATE / /

Today, I am grateful for: (starting with "I am grateful")

Now visualize each item, and say 'Thank you' three times as you read that gratitude back to affirm it.

GRATITUDE PROMPT

What unexpected blessings have come into my life recently?

As I reflect on yesterday, what went well, and what goals and/or learnings did I achieve?

My affirmations for today:

One thing that will make my day amazing today:

DATE / /

Today, I am grateful for: (starting with "I am grateful")

Now visualize each item, and say 'Thank you' three times as you read that gratitude back to affirm it.

GRATITUDE PROMPT

In what ways have I grown emotionally, mentally, or spiritually, and how am I grateful for this growth?

As I reflect on yesterday, what went well, and what goals and/or learnings did I achieve?

My affirmations for today:

One thing that will make my day amazing today:

DATE / /

Today, I am grateful for: (starting with "I am grateful")

Now visualize each item, and say 'Thank you' three times as you read that gratitude back to affirm it.

GRATITUDE PROMPT

What challenges have I faced recently, and what lessons have they taught me that I can be grateful for?

As I reflect on yesterday, what went well, and what goals and/or learnings did I achieve?

My affirmations for today:

One thing that will make my day amazing today:

DATE / /

Today, I am grateful for: (starting with "I am grateful")

Now visualize each item, and say 'Thank you' three times as you read that gratitude back to affirm it.

GRATITUDE PROMPT

What opportunities have I seized recently that I'm grateful for?

As I reflect on yesterday, what went well, and what goals and/or learnings did I achieve?

My affirmations for today:

One thing that will make my day amazing today:

DATE / /

Today, I am grateful for: (starting with "I am grateful")

Now visualize each item, and say 'Thank you' three times as you read that gratitude back to affirm it.

GRATITUDE PROMPT

Who have I connected with recently that has brought joy or inspiration into my life?

As I reflect on yesterday, what went well, and what goals and/or learnings did I achieve?

My affirmations for today:

One thing that will make my day amazing today:

DATE / /

Today, I am grateful for: (starting with "I am grateful")

Now visualize each item, and say 'Thank you' three times as you read that gratitude back to affirm it.

GRATITUDE PROMPT

What act of self-love will I commit to today?

As I reflect on yesterday, what went well, and what goals and/or learnings did I achieve?

My affirmations for today:

One thing that will make my day amazing today:

DATE / /

Today, I am grateful for: (starting with "I am grateful")

Now visualize each item, and say 'Thank you' three times as you read that gratitude back to affirm it.

GRATITUDE PROMPT

What moments of beauty or wonder have I experienced recently that I'm grateful for?

As I reflect on yesterday, what went well, and what goals and/or learnings did I achieve?

My affirmations for today:

One thing that will make my day amazing today:

DATE / /

Today, I am grateful for: (starting with "I am grateful")

Now visualize each item, and say 'Thank you' three times as you read that gratitude back to affirm it.

GRATITUDE PROMPT

What small acts of kindness have I received or witnessed that I'm grateful for?

As I reflect on yesterday, what went well, and what goals and/or learnings did I achieve?

My affirmations for today:

One thing that will make my day amazing today:

DATE / /

Today, I am grateful for: (starting with "I am grateful")

Now visualize each item, and say 'Thank you' three times as you read that gratitude back to affirm it.

GRATITUDE PROMPT

What progress have I made towards my goals, and how does that make me feel grateful?

As I reflect on yesterday, what went well, and what goals and/or learnings did I achieve?

My affirmations for today:

One thing that will make my day amazing today:

DATE / /

Today, I am grateful for: (starting with "I am grateful")

Now visualize each item, and say 'Thank you' three times as you read that gratitude back to affirm it.

GRATITUDE PROMPT

What talents or strengths do I possess that I'm grateful for?

As I reflect on yesterday, what went well, and what goals and/or learnings did I achieve?

My affirmations for today:

One thing that will make my day amazing today:

DATE / /

Today, I am grateful for: (starting with "I am grateful")

Now visualize each item, and say 'Thank you' three times as you read that gratitude back to affirm it.

GRATITUDE PROMPT

What opportunities for learning or personal development have I embraced recently?

As I reflect on yesterday, what went well, and what goals and/or learnings did I achieve?

My affirmations for today:

One thing that will make my day amazing today:

DATE / /

Today, I am grateful for: (starting with "I am grateful")

Now visualize each item, and say 'Thank you' three times as you read that gratitude back to affirm it.

GRATITUDE PROMPT

Who has inspired me recently, and what about them am I grateful for?

As I reflect on yesterday, what went well, and what goals and/or learnings did I achieve?

My affirmations for today:

One thing that will make my day amazing today:

DATE / /

Today, I am grateful for: (starting with "I am grateful")

Now visualize each item, and say 'Thank you' three times as you read that gratitude back to affirm it.

GRATITUDE PROMPT

How have I taken care of my physical, mental, or emotional well-being recently, and why am I grateful for this self-care?

As I reflect on yesterday, what went well, and what goals and/or learnings did I achieve?

My affirmations for today:

One thing that will make my day amazing today:

DATE / /

Today, I am grateful for: (starting with "I am grateful")

Now visualize each item, and say 'Thank you' three times as you read that gratitude back to affirm it.

GRATITUDE PROMPT

What opportunities for creativity or self-expression have I explored recently?

As I reflect on yesterday, what went well, and what goals and/or learnings did I achieve?

My affirmations for today:

One thing that will make my day amazing today:

DATE / /

Today, I am grateful for: (starting with "I am grateful")

Now visualize each item, and say 'Thank you' three times as you read that gratitude back to affirm it.

GRATITUDE PROMPT

What moments of clarity or insight have I experienced recently, and how have they guided me?

As I reflect on yesterday, what went well, and what goals and/or learnings did I achieve?

My affirmations for today:

One thing that will make my day amazing today:

DATE / /

Today, I am grateful for: (starting with "I am grateful")

Now visualize each item, and say 'Thank you' three times as you read that gratitude back to affirm it.

GRATITUDE PROMPT

How have I embraced uncertainty or change recently, and what positives have come from this openness?

As I reflect on yesterday, what went well, and what goals and/or learnings did I achieve?

My affirmations for today:

One thing that will make my day amazing today:

DATE / /

Today, I am grateful for: (starting with "I am grateful")

Now visualize each item, and say 'Thank you' three times as you read that gratitude back to affirm it.

GRATITUDE PROMPT

What recent experiences have deepened my sense of gratitude for life itself?

As I reflect on yesterday, what went well, and what goals and/or learnings did I achieve?

My affirmations for today:

One thing that will make my day amazing today:

DATE / /

Today, I am grateful for: (starting with "I am grateful")

Now visualize each item, and say 'Thank you' three times as you read that gratitude back to affirm it.

GRATITUDE PROMPT

What made me smile today, and why?

As I reflect on yesterday, what went well, and what goals and/or learnings did I achieve?

My affirmations for today:

One thing that will make my day amazing today:

DATE / /

Today, I am grateful for: (starting with "I am grateful")

-
-
-
-
-

Now visualize each item, and say 'Thank you' three times as you read that gratitude back to affirm it.

GRATITUDE PROMPT

How did nature nurture or provide solace for me today?

As I reflect on yesterday, what went well, and what goals and/or learnings did I achieve?

My affirmations for today:

One thing that will make my day amazing today:

DATE / /

Today, I am grateful for: (starting with "I am grateful")

Now visualize each item, and say 'Thank you' three times as you read that gratitude back to affirm it.

GRATITUDE PROMPT

What moments of peace or stillness did I find today, and how did they benefit me?

As I reflect on yesterday, what went well, and what goals and/or learnings did I achieve?

My affirmations for today:

One thing that will make my day amazing today:

DATE / /

Today, I am grateful for: (starting with "I am grateful")

Now visualize each item, and say 'Thank you' three times as you read that gratitude back to affirm it.

GRATITUDE PROMPT

How did I nourish my body, mind, or soul today, and why am I grateful for this nourishment?

As I reflect on yesterday, what went well, and what goals and/or learnings did I achieve?

My affirmations for today:

One thing that will make my day amazing today:

DATE / /

Today, I am grateful for: (starting with "I am grateful")

Now visualize each item, and say 'Thank you' three times as you read that gratitude back to affirm it.

GRATITUDE PROMPT

How did I cultivate a sense of abundance or prosperity in my life today?

As I reflect on yesterday, what went well, and what goals and/or learnings did I achieve?

My affirmations for today:

One thing that will make my day amazing today:

DATE / /

Today, I am grateful for: (starting with "I am grateful")

Now visualize each item, and say 'Thank you' three times as you read that gratitude back to affirm it.

GRATITUDE PROMPT

What simple pleasures did I enjoy today, and why am I grateful for them?

As I reflect on yesterday, what went well, and what goals and/or learnings did I achieve?

My affirmations for today:

One thing that will make my day amazing today:

DATE / /

Today, I am grateful for: (starting with "I am grateful")

Now visualize each item, and say 'Thank you' three times as you read that gratitude back to affirm it.

GRATITUDE PROMPT

What new opportunity am I grateful for today?

As I reflect on yesterday, what went well, and what goals and/or learnings did I achieve?

My affirmations for today:

One thing that will make my day amazing today:

DATE / /

Today, I am grateful for: (starting with "I am grateful")

Now visualize each item, and say 'Thank you' three times as you read that gratitude back to affirm it.

GRATITUDE PROMPT

What delicious meal or food experience am I grateful for today?

As I reflect on yesterday, what went well, and what goals and/or learnings did I achieve?

My affirmations for today:

One thing that will make my day amazing today:

DATE / /

Today, I am grateful for: (starting with "I am grateful")

Now visualize each item, and say 'Thank you' three times as you read that gratitude back to affirm it.

GRATITUDE PROMPT

Who shared an inspiring story or perspective with me today, and why am I grateful for that insight?

As I reflect on yesterday, what went well, and what goals and/or learnings did I achieve?

My affirmations for today:

One thing that will make my day amazing today:

DATE / /

Today, I am grateful for: (starting with "I am grateful")

Now visualize each item, and say 'Thank you' three times as you read that gratitude back to affirm it.

GRATITUDE PROMPT

What unexpected gesture of love or appreciation did I receive recently that I am grateful for?

As I reflect on yesterday, what went well, and what goals and/or learnings did I achieve?

My affirmations for today:

One thing that will make my day amazing today:

DATE / /

Today, I am grateful for: (starting with "I am grateful")

Now visualize each item, and say 'Thank you' three times as you read that gratitude back to affirm it.

GRATITUDE PROMPT

How did a recent experience deepen my sense of connection with others?

As I reflect on yesterday, what went well, and what goals and/or learnings did I achieve?

My affirmations for today:

One thing that will make my day amazing today:

Reflection Point

WHAT ARE YOUR THREE BIG MOMENTS SO FAR?

Many people tell us that after 30 days, they begin to sense a stronger connection to those around them. They also observe that their vibration is higher, and they notice small blessings come into their lives. The changes may not be huge to start with, but these blessings and moments continue to build and accumulate as they build their gratitude practice.

Think about the last 30 days of gratitude - what 3 things have you noticed about yourself and those around you?

If you want to kick it up a notch- Write to us at Manifestation Pulse (manifestationpulse@gmail.com) and tell us about these 3 observations. We'll treat your message like a postcard from the future and write back to remind of this in a few months so you're staying on track.

“Gratitude is riches.
Complaint is poverty.

- DORIS DAY

DATE / /

Today, I am grateful for: (starting with "I am grateful")

Now visualize each item, and say 'Thank you' three times as you read that gratitude back to affirm it.

GRATITUDE PROMPT

What small victory or achievement have I accomplished, and why am I grateful for that progress?

As I reflect on yesterday, what went well, and what goals and/or learnings did I achieve?

My affirmations for today:

One thing that will make my day amazing today:

DATE / /

Today, I am grateful for: (starting with "I am grateful")

Now visualize each item, and say 'Thank you' three times as you read that gratitude back to affirm it.

GRATITUDE PROMPT

What physical sensation or comfort brought me pleasure or relief today?

As I reflect on yesterday, what went well, and what goals and/or learnings did I achieve?

My affirmations for today:

One thing that will make my day amazing today:

DATE / /

Today, I am grateful for: (starting with "I am grateful")

Now visualize each item, and say 'Thank you' three times as you read that gratitude back to affirm it.

GRATITUDE PROMPT

What aspect of my environment or surroundings inspired a sense of wonder or awe?

As I reflect on yesterday, what went well, and what goals and/or learnings did I achieve?

My affirmations for today:

One thing that will make my day amazing today:

DATE / /

Today, I am grateful for: (starting with "I am grateful")

Now visualize each item, and say 'Thank you' three times as you read that gratitude back to affirm it.

GRATITUDE PROMPT

Has there been moment of serendipity or synchronicity that has made me smile recently?

As I reflect on yesterday, what went well, and what goals and/or learnings did I achieve?

My affirmations for today:

One thing that will make my day amazing today:

DATE / /

Today, I am grateful for: (starting with "I am grateful")

Now visualize each item, and say 'Thank you' three times as you read that gratitude back to affirm it.

GRATITUDE PROMPT

What cherished memory or nostalgic moment did I revisit recently, and why am I thankful for that?

As I reflect on yesterday, what went well, and what goals and/or learnings did I achieve?

My affirmations for today:

One thing that will make my day amazing today:

DATE / /

Today, I am grateful for: (starting with "I am grateful")

Now visualize each item, and say 'Thank you' three times as you read that gratitude back to affirm it.

GRATITUDE PROMPT

What aspect of my home or living space am I grateful for today?

As I reflect on yesterday, what went well, and what goals and/or learnings did I achieve?

My affirmations for today:

One thing that will make my day amazing today:

DATE / /

Today, I am grateful for: (starting with "I am grateful")

Now visualize each item, and say 'Thank you' three times as you read that gratitude back to affirm it.

GRATITUDE PROMPT

Do I feel a connection with the universe?
Why am I grateful for that?

As I reflect on yesterday, what went well, and what goals and/or learnings did I achieve?

My affirmations for today:

One thing that will make my day amazing today:

DATE / /

Today, I am grateful for: (starting with "I am grateful")

Now visualize each item, and say 'Thank you' three times as you read that gratitude back to affirm it.

GRATITUDE PROMPT

What opportunity for adventure or exploration did I embrace recently, and why am I thankful for that curiosity?

As I reflect on yesterday, what went well, and what goals and/or learnings did I achieve?

My affirmations for today:

One thing that will make my day amazing today:

DATE / /

Today, I am grateful for: (starting with "I am grateful")

Now visualize each item, and say 'Thank you' three times as you read that gratitude back to affirm it.

GRATITUDE PROMPT

What aspect of my professional life or career journey am I appreciating today?

As I reflect on yesterday, what went well, and what goals and/or learnings did I achieve?

My affirmations for today:

One thing that will make my day amazing today:

DATE / /

Today, I am grateful for: (starting with "I am grateful")

Now visualize each item, and say 'Thank you' three times as you read that gratitude back to affirm it.

GRATITUDE PROMPT

What aspect of my financial situation or material possessions am I appreciating today?

As I reflect on yesterday, what went well, and what goals and/or learnings did I achieve?

My affirmations for today:

One thing that will make my day amazing today:

DATE / /

Today, I am grateful for: (starting with "I am grateful")

Now visualize each item, and say 'Thank you' three times as you read that gratitude back to affirm it.

GRATITUDE PROMPT

Is there an aspect of my physical appearance or body that I am embracing and appreciating today? Why am I grateful for that self-acceptance?

As I reflect on yesterday, what went well, and what goals and/or learnings did I achieve?

My affirmations for today:

One thing that will make my day amazing today:

DATE / /

Today, I am grateful for: (starting with "I am grateful")

Now visualize each item, and say 'Thank you' three times as you read that gratitude back to affirm it.

GRATITUDE PROMPT

Has there been an opportunity for rest or relaxation that I prioritized today, and why am I grateful for that rejuvenation?

As I reflect on yesterday, what went well, and what goals and/or learnings did I achieve?

My affirmations for today:

One thing that will make my day amazing today:

DATE / /

Today, I am grateful for: (starting with "I am grateful")

Now visualize each item, and say 'Thank you' three times as you read that gratitude back to affirm it.

GRATITUDE PROMPT

What aspect of my cultural heritage or ancestry have I honored and celebrated recently that I am grateful for?

As I reflect on yesterday, what went well, and what goals and/or learnings did I achieve?

My affirmations for today:

One thing that will make my day amazing today:

DATE / /

Today, I am grateful for: (starting with "I am grateful")

Now visualize each item, and say 'Thank you' three times as you read that gratitude back to affirm it.

GRATITUDE PROMPT

In what ways did a recent experience foster a sense of gratitude for the gift of life itself?

As I reflect on yesterday, what went well, and what goals and/or learnings did I achieve?

My affirmations for today:

One thing that will make my day amazing today:

DATE / /

Today, I am grateful for: (starting with "I am grateful")

Now visualize each item, and say 'Thank you' three times as you read that gratitude back to affirm it.

GRATITUDE PROMPT

What aspect of my personality or character am I appreciating and embracing today, and why am I grateful for that authenticity?

As I reflect on yesterday, what went well, and what goals and/or learnings did I achieve?

My affirmations for today:

One thing that will make my day amazing today:

DATE / /

Today, I am grateful for: (starting with "I am grateful")

Now visualize each item, and say 'Thank you' three times as you read that gratitude back to affirm it.

GRATITUDE PROMPT

What have I learned recently that makes me grateful for that knowledge?

As I reflect on yesterday, what went well, and what goals and/or learnings did I achieve?

My affirmations for today:

One thing that will make my day amazing today:

DATE / /

Today, I am grateful for: (starting with "I am grateful")

Now visualize each item, and say 'Thank you' three times as you read that gratitude back to affirm it.

GRATITUDE PROMPT

In what ways have I seen the importance of self-reflection, and why am I grateful for that introspection?

As I reflect on yesterday, what went well, and what goals and/or learnings did I achieve?

My affirmations for today:

One thing that will make my day amazing today:

DATE / /

Today, I am grateful for: (starting with "I am grateful")

Now visualize each item, and say 'Thank you' three times as you read that gratitude back to affirm it.

GRATITUDE PROMPT

What part of my daily routine or ritual brought me comfort recently, and why am I grateful for that consistency?

As I reflect on yesterday, what went well, and what goals and/or learnings did I achieve?

My affirmations for today:

One thing that will make my day amazing today:

DATE / /

Today, I am grateful for: (starting with "I am grateful")

Now visualize each item, and say 'Thank you' three times as you read that gratitude back to affirm it.

GRATITUDE PROMPT

How have I been challenged to step outside of my comfort zone?

As I reflect on yesterday, what went well, and what goals and/or learnings did I achieve?

My affirmations for today:

One thing that will make my day amazing today:

DATE / /

Today, I am grateful for: (starting with "I am grateful")

Now visualize each item, and say 'Thank you' three times as you read that gratitude back to affirm it.

GRATITUDE PROMPT

In what ways did recent experiences deepen my sense of gratitude for the interconnectedness of all living beings?

As I reflect on yesterday, what went well, and what goals and/or learnings did I achieve?

My affirmations for today:

One thing that will make my day amazing today:

DATE / /

Today, I am grateful for: (starting with "I am grateful")

Now visualize each item, and say 'Thank you' three times as you read that gratitude back to affirm it.

GRATITUDE PROMPT

How did recent experiences remind me of the importance of forgiveness, and why am I grateful for that healing?

As I reflect on yesterday, what went well, and what goals and/or learnings did I achieve?

My affirmations for today:

One thing that will make my day amazing today:

DATE / /

Today, I am grateful for: (starting with "I am grateful")

Now visualize each item, and say 'Thank you' three times as you read that gratitude back to affirm it.

GRATITUDE PROMPT

Who has given me a profound uplift or level of support that I am truly grateful for?

As I reflect on yesterday, what went well, and what goals and/or learnings did I achieve?

My affirmations for today:

One thing that will make my day amazing today:

DATE / /

Today, I am grateful for: (starting with "I am grateful")

Now visualize each item, and say 'Thank you' three times as you read that gratitude back to affirm it.

GRATITUDE PROMPT

How did recent experiences deepen my sense of gratitude for the power of love and connection in my life?

As I reflect on yesterday, what went well, and what goals and/or learnings did I achieve?

My affirmations for today:

One thing that will make my day amazing today:

DATE / /

Today, I am grateful for: (starting with "I am grateful")

Now visualize each item, and say 'Thank you' three times as you read that gratitude back to affirm it.

GRATITUDE PROMPT

In what ways did recent experiences remind me of the importance of self-love and self-compassion, and why am I grateful for that acceptance?

As I reflect on yesterday, what went well, and what goals and/or learnings did I achieve?

My affirmations for today:

One thing that will make my day amazing today:

DATE / /

Today, I am grateful for: (starting with "I am grateful")

Now visualize each item, and say 'Thank you' three times as you read that gratitude back to affirm it.

GRATITUDE PROMPT

What small victory or accomplishment can I celebrate, and why am I grateful for that progress?

As I reflect on yesterday, what went well, and what goals and/or learnings did I achieve?

My affirmations for today:

One thing that will make my day amazing today:

DATE / /

Today, I am grateful for: (starting with "I am grateful")

Now visualize each item, and say 'Thank you' three times as you read that gratitude back to affirm it.

GRATITUDE PROMPT

In what ways did recent experiences deepen my sense of gratitude for the resilience and adaptability of my spirit?

As I reflect on yesterday, what went well, and what goals and/or learnings did I achieve?

My affirmations for today:

One thing that will make my day amazing today:

DATE / /

Today, I am grateful for: (starting with "I am grateful")

Now visualize each item, and say 'Thank you' three times as you read that gratitude back to affirm it.

GRATITUDE PROMPT

What experiences that have deepened my sense of gratitude for the power of community and collaboration?

As I reflect on yesterday, what went well, and what goals and/or learnings did I achieve?

My affirmations for today:

One thing that will make my day amazing today:

DATE / /

Today, I am grateful for: (starting with "I am grateful")

Now visualize each item, and say 'Thank you' three times as you read that gratitude back to affirm it.

GRATITUDE PROMPT

What aspect of my emotional well-being am I appreciating and enjoying, and why am I grateful for that inner peace?

As I reflect on yesterday, what went well, and what goals and/or learnings did I achieve?

My affirmations for today:

One thing that will make my day amazing today:

DATE / /

Today, I am grateful for: (starting with "I am grateful")

Now visualize each item, and say 'Thank you' three times as you read that gratitude back to affirm it.

GRATITUDE PROMPT

In what ways did recent experiences remind me of the importance of gratitude in fostering positive relationships with others?

As I reflect on yesterday, what went well, and what goals and/or learnings did I achieve?

My affirmations for today:

One thing that will make my day amazing today:

DATE / /

Today, I am grateful for: (starting with "I am grateful")

Now visualize each item, and say 'Thank you' three times as you read that gratitude back to affirm it.

GRATITUDE PROMPT

How did a setback or challenge provide me with opportunities for growth and learning, and why am I thankful for those lessons?

As I reflect on yesterday, what went well, and what goals and/or learnings did I achieve?

My affirmations for today:

One thing that will make my day amazing today:

Reflection Point

DESCRIBE SOMETHING IN YOUR LIFE THAT YOU HAVE NOW BUT ONLY DREAMT OF HAVING IN THE PAST.

Over time, we achieve goals, make our desires come true, and ultimately grow. We move on to the next desire quickly, sometimes forgetting that the progress we've made in the past 60 days of gratitude was once just a dream. So take a moment to reflect on on your progress right now.

“

Gratitude and love are always multiplied when you give freely. It is an infinite source of contentment and prosperous energy.

- JIM FARGIANO

”

DATE / /

Today, I am grateful for: (starting with "I am grateful")

Now visualize each item, and say 'Thank you' three times as you read that gratitude back to affirm it.

GRATITUDE PROMPT

Have I had recent interactions with strangers or acquaintances that reminded me of the importance of kindness and compassion?

As I reflect on yesterday, what went well, and what goals and/or learnings did I achieve?

My affirmations for today:

One thing that will make my day amazing today:

DATE / /

Today, I am grateful for: (starting with "I am grateful")

Now visualize each item, and say 'Thank you' three times as you read that gratitude back to affirm it.

GRATITUDE PROMPT

What adventure or exploration did I embrace recently, and why am I thankful for that?

As I reflect on yesterday, what went well, and what goals and/or learnings did I achieve?

My affirmations for today:

One thing that will make my day amazing today:

DATE / /

Today, I am grateful for: (starting with "I am grateful")

Now visualize each item, and say 'Thank you' three times as you read that gratitude back to affirm it.

GRATITUDE PROMPT

What aspect of my inner strength or resilience did I tap into recently, and why am I grateful for that courage?

As I reflect on yesterday, what went well, and what goals and/or learnings did I achieve?

My affirmations for today:

One thing that will make my day amazing today:

DATE / /

Today, I am grateful for: (starting with "I am grateful")

Now visualize each item, and say 'Thank you' three times as you read that gratitude back to affirm it.

GRATITUDE PROMPT

What aspect of my emotional well-being am I appreciating and enjoying recently?

As I reflect on yesterday, what went well, and what goals and/or learnings did I achieve?

My affirmations for today:

One thing that will make my day amazing today:

DATE / /

Today, I am grateful for: (starting with "I am grateful")

Now visualize each item, and say 'Thank you' three times as you read that gratitude back to affirm it.

GRATITUDE PROMPT

In which ways have I unleashed my imagination recently that I am thankful for?

As I reflect on yesterday, what went well, and what goals and/or learnings did I achieve?

My affirmations for today:

One thing that will make my day amazing today:

DATE / /

Today, I am grateful for: (starting with "I am grateful")

Now visualize each item, and say 'Thank you' three times as you read that gratitude back to affirm it.

GRATITUDE PROMPT

Have I had a recent experience around the gift of health and well-being, and if so, why am I thankful for that vitality?

As I reflect on yesterday, what went well, and what goals and/or learnings did I achieve?

My affirmations for today:

One thing that will make my day amazing today:

DATE / /

Today, I am grateful for: (starting with "I am grateful")

Now visualize each item, and say 'Thank you' three times as you read that gratitude back to affirm it.

GRATITUDE PROMPT

Has there been a newer spiritual practice or belief I am appreciating and enjoying recently?

As I reflect on yesterday, what went well, and what goals and/or learnings did I achieve?

My affirmations for today:

One thing that will make my day amazing today:

DATE / /

Today, I am grateful for: (starting with "I am grateful")

Now visualize each item, and say 'Thank you' three times as you read that gratitude back to affirm it.

GRATITUDE PROMPT

What recent experience has fostered a sense of resilience and perseverance?

As I reflect on yesterday, what went well, and what goals and/or learnings did I achieve?

My affirmations for today:

One thing that will make my day amazing today:

DATE / /

Today, I am grateful for: (starting with "I am grateful")

Now visualize each item, and say 'Thank you' three times as you read that gratitude back to affirm it.

GRATITUDE PROMPT

How have I been adaptable to new change recently?

As I reflect on yesterday, what went well, and what goals and/or learnings did I achieve?

My affirmations for today:

One thing that will make my day amazing today:

DATE / /

Today, I am grateful for: (starting with "I am grateful")

Now visualize each item, and say 'Thank you' three times as you read that gratitude back to affirm it.

GRATITUDE PROMPT

Is there an item or element of my home that I have never fully appreciated until today?

As I reflect on yesterday, what went well, and what goals and/or learnings did I achieve?

My affirmations for today:

One thing that will make my day amazing today:

DATE / /

Today, I am grateful for: (starting with "I am grateful")

Now visualize each item, and say 'Thank you' three times as you read that gratitude back to affirm it.

GRATITUDE PROMPT

Is there someone who has surprised me by their level of support and dedication in my life?

As I reflect on yesterday, what went well, and what goals and/or learnings did I achieve?

My affirmations for today:

One thing that will make my day amazing today:

DATE / /

Today, I am grateful for: (starting with "I am grateful")

Now visualize each item, and say 'Thank you' three times as you read that gratitude back to affirm it.

GRATITUDE PROMPT

What have I seen recently that has genuinely amazed me?

As I reflect on yesterday, what went well, and what goals and/or learnings did I achieve?

My affirmations for today:

One thing that will make my day amazing today:

DATE / /

Today, I am grateful for: (starting with "I am grateful")

Now visualize each item, and say 'Thank you' three times as you read that gratitude back to affirm it.

GRATITUDE PROMPT

What joy or laughter have I shared with others recently, and why am I thankful for that camaraderie?

As I reflect on yesterday, what went well, and what goals and/or learnings did I achieve?

My affirmations for today:

One thing that will make my day amazing today:

DATE / /

Today, I am grateful for: (starting with "I am grateful")

Now visualize each item, and say 'Thank you' three times as you read that gratitude back to affirm it.

GRATITUDE PROMPT

What setbacks have I had that have actually provided a totally new perspective for growth?

As I reflect on yesterday, what went well, and what goals and/or learnings did I achieve?

My affirmations for today:

One thing that will make my day amazing today:

DATE / /

Today, I am grateful for: (starting with "I am grateful")

Now visualize each item, and say 'Thank you' three times as you read that gratitude back to affirm it.

GRATITUDE PROMPT

What is something that I have taken for granted previously that I now want to be truly thankful for?

As I reflect on yesterday, what went well, and what goals and/or learnings did I achieve?

My affirmations for today:

One thing that will make my day amazing today:

DATE / /

Today, I am grateful for: (starting with "I am grateful")

Now visualize each item, and say 'Thank you' three times as you read that gratitude back to affirm it.

GRATITUDE PROMPT

How did I recently replenish my energy in a way that I can be thankful for?

As I reflect on yesterday, what went well, and what goals and/or learnings did I achieve?

My affirmations for today:

One thing that will make my day amazing today:

DATE / /

Today, I am grateful for: (starting with "I am grateful")

Now visualize each item, and say 'Thank you' three times as you read that gratitude back to affirm it.

GRATITUDE PROMPT

What simple thing in nature can I be thankful for? E.g. the sun that helps my plants grow?

As I reflect on yesterday, what went well, and what goals and/or learnings did I achieve?

My affirmations for today:

One thing that will make my day amazing today:

DATE / /

Today, I am grateful for: (starting with "I am grateful")

Now visualize each item, and say 'Thank you' three times as you read that gratitude back to affirm it.

GRATITUDE PROMPT

What part of my mind and/or body am I particularly proud of? E.g. I am proud of my strong and powerful lungs that give me fresh air throughout my body.

As I reflect on yesterday, what went well, and what goals and/or learnings did I achieve?

My affirmations for today:

One thing that will make my day amazing today:

DATE / /

Today, I am grateful for: (starting with "I am grateful")

Now visualize each item, and say 'Thank you' three times as you read that gratitude back to affirm it.

GRATITUDE PROMPT

What moment of inner peace and clarity have I had recently that I am thankful for?

As I reflect on yesterday, what went well, and what goals and/or learnings did I achieve?

My affirmations for today:

One thing that will make my day amazing today:

DATE / /

Today, I am grateful for: (starting with "I am grateful")

Now visualize each item, and say 'Thank you' three times as you read that gratitude back to affirm it.

GRATITUDE PROMPT

Have I been creative in overcoming a problem that I am grateful for?

As I reflect on yesterday, what went well, and what goals and/or learnings did I achieve?

My affirmations for today:

One thing that will make my day amazing today:

DATE / /

Today, I am grateful for: (starting with "I am grateful")

Now visualize each item, and say 'Thank you' three times as you read that gratitude back to affirm it.

GRATITUDE PROMPT

What aspect of my culture or background has given me a new perspective on gratefulness?

As I reflect on yesterday, what went well, and what goals and/or learnings did I achieve?

My affirmations for today:

One thing that will make my day amazing today:

DATE / /

Today, I am grateful for: (starting with "I am grateful")

Now visualize each item, and say 'Thank you' three times as you read that gratitude back to affirm it.

GRATITUDE PROMPT

How have I been included in something recently that I am thankful for?

As I reflect on yesterday, what went well, and what goals and/or learnings did I achieve?

My affirmations for today:

One thing that will make my day amazing today:

DATE / /

Today, I am grateful for: (starting with "I am grateful")

Now visualize each item, and say 'Thank you' three times as you read that gratitude back to affirm it.

GRATITUDE PROMPT

Have my powers of resilience been tested to the point where I can be grateful?

As I reflect on yesterday, what went well, and what goals and/or learnings did I achieve?

My affirmations for today:

One thing that will make my day amazing today:

DATE / /

Today, I am grateful for: (starting with "I am grateful")

Now visualize each item, and say 'Thank you' three times as you read that gratitude back to affirm it.

GRATITUDE PROMPT

What unexpected gesture of love or appreciation did I receive recently, and why does it fill my heart with gratitude?

As I reflect on yesterday, what went well, and what goals and/or learnings did I achieve?

My affirmations for today:

One thing that will make my day amazing today:

DATE / /

Today, I am grateful for: (starting with "I am grateful")

Now visualize each item, and say 'Thank you' three times as you read that gratitude back to affirm it.

GRATITUDE PROMPT

What small victory or achievement am I celebrating today, and why am I grateful for that progress?

As I reflect on yesterday, what went well, and what goals and/or learnings did I achieve?

My affirmations for today:

One thing that will make my day amazing today:

DATE / /

Today, I am grateful for: (starting with "I am grateful")

Now visualize each item, and say 'Thank you' three times as you read that gratitude back to affirm it.

GRATITUDE PROMPT

How did I show kindness or make a positive impact on someone else's life recently?

As I reflect on yesterday, what went well, and what goals and/or learnings did I achieve?

My affirmations for today:

One thing that will make my day amazing today:

DATE / /

Today, I am grateful for: (starting with "I am grateful")

Now visualize each item, and say 'Thank you' three times as you read that gratitude back to affirm it.

GRATITUDE PROMPT

Who did I connect with recently that brought joy or inspiration into my life?

As I reflect on yesterday, what went well, and what goals and/or learnings did I achieve?

My affirmations for today:

One thing that will make my day amazing today:

DATE / /

Today, I am grateful for: (starting with "I am grateful")

Now visualize each item, and say 'Thank you' three times as you read that gratitude back to affirm it.

GRATITUDE PROMPT

Did nature nurture or provide solace for me recently?

As I reflect on yesterday, what went well, and what goals and/or learnings did I achieve?

My affirmations for today:

One thing that will make my day amazing today:

DATE / /

Today, I am grateful for: (starting with "I am grateful")

Now visualize each item, and say 'Thank you' three times as you read that gratitude back to affirm it.

GRATITUDE PROMPT

How did I contribute to creating a positive environment for myself or others, and why am I grateful for this?

As I reflect on yesterday, what went well, and what goals and/or learnings did I achieve?

My affirmations for today:

One thing that will make my day amazing today:

DATE / /

Today, I am grateful for: (starting with "I am grateful")

Now visualize each item, and say 'Thank you' three times as you read that gratitude back to affirm it.

GRATITUDE PROMPT

What achievements can I express gratitude towards, or acknowledge my own success for?

As I reflect on yesterday, what went well, and what goals and/or learnings did I achieve?

My affirmations for today:

One thing that will make my day amazing today:

DATE / /

Today, I am grateful for: (starting with "I am grateful")

Now visualize each item, and say 'Thank you' three times as you read that gratitude back to affirm it.

GRATITUDE PROMPT

What talents or strengths did I utilize recently that I'm grateful for?

As I reflect on yesterday, what went well, and what goals and/or learnings did I achieve?

My affirmations for today:

One thing that will make my day amazing today:

DATE / /

Today, I am grateful for: (starting with "I am grateful")

Now visualize each item, and say 'Thank you' three times as you read that gratitude back to affirm it.

GRATITUDE PROMPT

Who or what made me smile recently, and why?

As I reflect on yesterday, what went well, and what goals and/or learnings did I achieve?

My affirmations for today:

One thing that will make my day amazing today:

DATE / /

Today, I am grateful for: (starting with "I am grateful")

Now visualize each item, and say 'Thank you' three times as you read that gratitude back to affirm it.

GRATITUDE PROMPT

How did practicing gratitude positively impact my day yesterday?

As I reflect on yesterday, what went well, and what goals and/or learnings did I achieve?

My affirmations for today:

One thing that will make my day amazing today:

DATE / /

Today, I am grateful for: (starting with "I am grateful")

Now visualize each item, and say 'Thank you' three times as you read that gratitude back to affirm it.

GRATITUDE PROMPT

What moments of beauty or wonder have I experienced that I'm grateful for?

As I reflect on yesterday, what went well, and what goals and/or learnings did I achieve?

My affirmations for today:

One thing that will make my day amazing today:

DATE / /

Today, I am grateful for: (starting with "I am grateful")

Now visualize each item, and say 'Thank you' three times as you read that gratitude back to affirm it.

GRATITUDE PROMPT

What is something that makes me truly unique that I can be grateful for?

As I reflect on yesterday, what went well, and what goals and/or learnings did I achieve?

My affirmations for today:

One thing that will make my day amazing today:

DATE / /

Today, I am grateful for: (starting with "I am grateful")

Now visualize each item, and say 'Thank you' three times as you read that gratitude back to affirm it.

GRATITUDE PROMPT

What intentions or affirmations did I set, and how do they inspire feelings of gratitude and empowerment?

As I reflect on yesterday, what went well, and what goals and/or learnings did I achieve?

My affirmations for today:

One thing that will make my day amazing today:

DATE / /

Today, I am grateful for: (starting with "I am grateful")

Now visualize each item, and say 'Thank you' three times as you read that gratitude back to affirm it.

GRATITUDE PROMPT

How have I shown kindness or made a positive impact on someone else's life recently?

As I reflect on yesterday, what went well, and what goals and/or learnings did I achieve?

My affirmations for today:

One thing that will make my day amazing today:

DATE / /

Today, I am grateful for: (starting with "I am grateful")

Now visualize each item, and say 'Thank you' three times as you read that gratitude back to affirm it.

GRATITUDE PROMPT

What dreams or aspirations have I pursued recently, and how does this make me feel grateful for my ambition?

As I reflect on yesterday, what went well, and what goals and/or learnings did I achieve?

My affirmations for today:

One thing that will make my day amazing today:

DATE / /

Today, I am grateful for: (starting with "I am grateful")

Now visualize each item, and say 'Thank you' three times as you read that gratitude back to affirm it.

GRATITUDE PROMPT

What unexpected moments have come into my life recently that I am grateful for?

As I reflect on yesterday, what went well, and what goals and/or learnings did I achieve?

My affirmations for today:

One thing that will make my day amazing today:

DATE / /

Today, I am grateful for: (starting with "I am grateful")

Now visualize each item, and say 'Thank you' three times as you read that gratitude back to affirm it.

GRATITUDE PROMPT

How has practicing gratitude positively impacted my mindset or overall well-being?

As I reflect on yesterday, what went well, and what goals and/or learnings did I achieve?

My affirmations for today:

One thing that will make my day amazing today:

Reflection Point

NOT THE END, BUT THE CONTINUING START OF YOUR JOURNEY.

Remember when you first started this journal? You probably had a lot of hopes, but also some doubts about what was possible. While you knew gratitude was important, your relationship to it will have grown and evolved over the time spent actually practicing it. As you come to the end of these first 100 days, how far have you come?

“

Whatever you appreciate and give thanks for will increase in your life.

- SANAYA ROMAN

”

Your Gift

AS A THANK YOU FOR GETTING THIS JOURNAL WE'D LIKE TO ALSO OFFER YOU:
SCAN THE CODE TO GET YOUR COPY

100 GRATITUDE PROMPTS:
Keep your gratitude habit as powerful as possible with this mini book of amazing gratitude prompts.

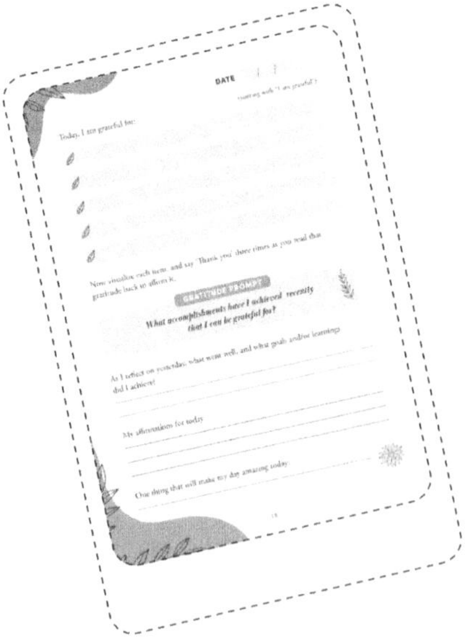

MORE GRATITUDE TEMPLATES :
Keep your gratitude habit going with even more daily templates for you to use.